CW00404708

Sleeping With You

and other night-time adventures

Geoff Stevens

Indigo Dreams Publishing

First Edition: Geoff Stevens
First published in Great Britain in 2012 by:
Indigo Dreams Publishing
132 Hinckley Road
Stoney Stanton
Leicestershire
LE9 4LN

www.indigodreams.co.uk

ISBN 978-1-907401-61-9

British Library Cataloguing in Publication Data. A CIP record for this book can be obtained from the British Library.

Designed and typeset in Palatino Linotype by Indigo Dreams.

Cover design by Ronnie Goodyer at Indigo Dreams.

Cover image by Geraldine Wall.

Printed and bound in Great Britain by Imprint Academic, Exeter.

To Geraldine

Acknowledgements

Some of these poems have appeared in:

4th Dimension; Absinthe On Your Ice-cream; Chiron Review (USA); Erete's Bloom; Essence; Ink, Sweat &Tears(Internet); Konfluence; The Moon (USA); Quarry; Red Owl(USA); Solo Survivors Anthology; Swansea International Poetry Festival anthology; The Fractal Translight Newsletter (USA);Tule Review (USA); Waterways (USA); Write Out Loud (Internet).

Previous Poetry Publications

Ecstasy (Krax) 1992
Field Manual For Poetry Lovers (K.T.Publications) 1992
A Comparison Of Myself With Ivan Blatny (Magic Pen Press) 1992
The Surreal Mind Paints Poetry (Michael Green) 1993
The Complacency Of The English (Wonderhorn) 1995
For Reference Only (Poetry Monthly Press) 1999
Been There (Poetry Monthly Press) 1999
At The Edge/Central To Me (Spouting Forth Ink) 1999
with Wayne Dean-Richards
Favourite Trax (Brendan Hawthorne) 2003
with Brendan Hawthorne.
The Phrenology Of Anaglypta (Bluechrome) 2004
A Keelhauling Through Ireland (Poetry Monthly Press) 2005
The All Night Café (Poetry Wednesbury Publications) 2006
with Brendan Hawthorne
Reality Is Not Achievable (The Moon Publishing, USA) 2006
Absinthe On Your Ice-Cream (Poetry Monthly Press) 2007
Previously Uncollected Selected Poems 1974-2007
(Poetry Monthly Press) 2008
The Instability of Nitro-Cellulose (Last Chance
Before Bedtime) 2009
Islands In The Blood (Indigo Dreams Publishing) 2010

CONTENTS

Sleeping With You

and other night-time adventures

THE PLOUGH & OTHER CONSTERNATIONS

the way to grandma's house
is a waste land of ancient dandelions
brown-rimmed clover flowers
cow-parsley skeletons
illuminated by the moon
and by the shy sly winking stars
trying to seduce me
into their black black satin sky

FIRST STEPS

I am in damp pink-striped pyjamas
and the sides of my cot
surround me like spiked-top iron railings
Hot and breathless the darkness
oscillates like a park swing squeaking
I can smell the burnt-out shell
of the wax night-light candle
hear the spluttering of the fire's coal-gas
the wheezing of my accordion chest
Pneumonia the doctor said
double pneumonia
the boy should be dead
Teddy bear under one arm
I sleep walk in my dream-filled bed

SUNSET, BLEAKLOW

Gone the shadows
sculpting their grit-stone grotesques
next to the burning of the sun,
where the lizard isotherms his blood,
the honey-scent of heather,
taste-buds sharpened by the bilberry bite.
We are with the short end of the spectrum now
and sunset over Bleaklow
blackens the earth,
makes mauve the snow.

SUNSET AND MATCH

Eyes starry, and pointing to the Pole
you enfold me
like a warm summer night
the fireflies sparking from your hair
cloy me in your embrace
our breaths squeezed out
as night air diminishes
in our busy mouths.
And we ignite
a naked breeze cooling the sweat
upon our brows
your eager hands
glued around my neck.
And behind all this
our horizon is a last touch of fire
like a trace of strontium
on a spectrograph
crimson in its desire to propagate.

GLANCE

We had each other
well before we went to bed

we touched
before we even touched

I saw it in your eyes
as we were doing it

the wondering if
we should repeat it

in the flesh

DISMEMBERED BY DARKNESS

Dismembered by darkness
and black clothing,
her face, hands, legs
shine like neon,
whilst his fingers work urgently
to join up the pieces,
unfastening buttons and hooks, unzipping frantically.

SLEEPING WITH YOU

I want thoughts of me
to sleep with you
before I do.
I want to walk your dreams
stalk your desires
in the throes of Morpheus,
for images to scream
in your day dreams
of us together.
I want you to sleep on the future
so that when it happens
we will share the new awakening
of pleasure.
Just murmur my name at midnight
and although I won't hear you
I will come.

THE ALL-NIGHT CAFFEINE

No espresso for me
I want to be kept awake to all opportunity
throughout the darkened hours
my nerve ends tingling
pricked with energy
the warmth of alkaloidal stimulation
percolating to my loins
with all the Brazilian-style thrill
of midnight skinny-dipping
on the Copacabana.

NIGHT WINDOW

the darkness

the drizzle

the traffic lights

stuck on red

a knowing blink

of night

shining in

embarrassing

the wallpaper

LOVERS

This is the vacuum of the day
night takes the light
and you with your superior tugging strength
take the duvet away
with your extra lung capacity
breathe all my air
Please turn down your heartbeats
you are ruining my silence
upsetting my sleep
and your dreams are infringing on my dreams
Keep to your own side
you're giving me claustrophobia
your elbows are weird
they have four sharp bones on them
you're bruising my ribs
your snoring's out of tune
it's upsetting the regularity of my breathing
you'll bring on my angina.
WHAT NOW!
No, I don't feel like it.
I don't want a cheese sandwich.
You have one if you want one
and don't keep asking me things
can't you see
I'm asleep!

Snoring is a sort of fog warning.
It stops vessels from bumping in to each other
in the night.

ALMOST STRANGERS

I lay awake last night
wondering what it would be like
with you
and now I'm here
and you're not at all shy
she said
taking off her jeans
as if she'd spilled hot coffee
over them.
And there's something about the way
that women cross their arms
to lift their sweaters off
that fascinates a man.
And though there wasn't much
of her beneath
she was lithe
had movement like a snake
a constrictor that held on for grim death
and poisonous too
went for me both tooth and nail
I've got the marks to prove it
on my skin.

Afterwards I wondered if she'd come again
and when a few nights later
I heard the determined knocking of her passion
in my heart
I felt I had to let her in.

VAMP

Once it was violent to me
went for the jugular
hit me without saying why
then walked away
leaving a black I

and me to cure my heart
with a raw stake
driven right through with guilt
one of the living dead
with a sermon in my head

coffin for a bed
and dreams that walked at night
your shadow stalking me
the smile before those teeth
sank into me

tearing myself away from me.
But love is a pleasure
now that you've changed your ways
so tell me, my love, was it the cross?
Or the garlic on my breath?

AVICULA

Darkness permits you
to traverse the room
with modesty
and climb into the bed
where I in my oyster
await the return
of the single pearl earring
that is your only adornment.

NOCTHANKEROUS

The dream is empty
a nightdress of flesh
draped over a bed
its nylon woman
lying discarded
on the floor

KERNAL SANDERS *and*
the apportioning of other
depraved acts of late night
entertainment

Roasting him over old flames
basting him with taunts
searing his skin with cruel barbs
blistering him with her acid tongue
slitting his flesh with her fingernails
sticking the knife in
cutting through his ribs
with jaw-like secateurs
plucking out his offal
and feeding it to the cat
tearing off about a leg-over situations
and letting the juices
run down her chin
consuming his flesh
and putting his bones in a cardboard box
and leaving them in a bus shelter.

Just another Saturday night out down the club
followed by the obligatory take-away.

NIGHT SERVICE

On the late bus
the atmosphere breathes from the stomach
ingested beer and curry
and you sit in the leering zone
showing too much leg in your short skirt
while the legless lager-louts
utter their desires
The blackboarded streets
chalked with their darkest menus
press against the windows
vagrant diners
looking out from the shadows
and pleading to be let in
to escape from the impending violence.

NIGHT SCENTED STOCK

In the florist's shop at night
the flowers are having a social drink
are having a chat
recalling lost friends
joking and sometimes bragging
of the big noses that have thrust themselves
amongst their petals
recalling their earth homes
wild places
gardens and greenhouses
and getting a little tipsy
rambling on
or drooping a little
falling off their stems
or settling down to sleeping it off
hoping to be bright and perky
looking their best
for a fresh tomorrow

ANEMONE

The dream was dark
lit only by a candle moon
as smoky as a charcoal burner's oven
but cold
and then there was the wind and rain
briskly changing tack
like a flock of starlings
or a pistol whipping with wet branches
in a storm
and I heard you call
looked and saw
you standing naked in a clearing
all that weak lunar luminescence
concentrating on your flesh
so that it glared like limelight
before it disappeared
into the velvet darkness
of my wooded mind
through the image
branded on the eye
like a glowing tungsten twist
a ghostly filament of the imagination
only to reappear in another place
amongst the foliage
And so it went
Was I naked too?
I couldn't tell
I could not see myself
but the sharp wet branches slashed my skin
as though I was
It was a frantic game of chase
plus hide and seek
which ended when simultaneously we woke

within a blizzard of twisted sheets
my hands clasped around your wrists
and the bed full of sodden leaves.

BATTLEDORE

Their shared dreams take place
on the midnight lawn
where in the stillness of moonlight
each in their nightdresses
and holding a racket of cat gut
that calls in the night
to a cock
that shuttles from one to the other
each wanting to secure it
but foiled by the tautness of it all
from heartstrings to heartstrings
sister to sister
it pendulums the night
to the frustration of both
so that at breakfast
neither will pass the butter
until the young man
asks

BETWEEN FORTUNESWELL
AND LANGTON HERRING

You walk barefoot in your dreams
take penance over pebbles that stretch
as far as the tilting sky
it is much the same as walking Chesil in the daytime
except that when you are on Chesil Beach
you always know how far you are
by the size of the stones
whereas in your sleep
you become lost because the stones are
all the same size
are all as sharp
all as hard
you are frightened
shout out in anguish and despair
there is no end to penance
no cool pool of Abbotsbury
with white swans gliding peacefully
no end to the nightmare

BAD NIGHTS IN BEDLAM

Night exists only in
the mind switched off
imagination
of places away
from the walls and whispers

from the pollutions of light
that stand up on stalks
of electricity

night is not the barking
of the midnight sun
but a bleating
within sleep's dreams

a grey disembowelment
silent and scabied

Its car journeys
are without drivers
are halogen lasers
glowing like furnace steel
that wrap themselves around towns
by convulsion

They share their noise
with invisible train schedules
that peer out of timetables
with welder's eye

Night is the smudged printing
on the pages
It is written within our minds

through inbreeding
is a vanished phenomenon
dazed with concussion's stars

It blinks between legend
and reality
waits for the sun
to put its eye out

SEDUCED BY THE SINGER LE MANS

Driving at night
between bottle-green pine trees
on top of the world
the darkness splattering on the windscreen
its headlight moon
swerving at the last moment
before collision
and killing an unknown badger
out for the evening
beneath the blipping neon radar
of the stars
your heart beating louder
than Serge Gainsbourg
singing Ballade de Melody Nelson
on the radio
while the distant town lights
hover like fireflies
that will never get closer
as my hand on your thigh
you pull over
and switch on my engine.

TRAGIC HEROINE

Light beams
from the headlights of cars
pierce the window
plough through the darkness of the room
as you try to break free from your nightmare dreams
your mind-figure running free in see-through escape gear
silhouetted and shot down sobbing
as wakened by your distress
I take you in my arms.

DRIVING THOUGHTS

Midnight
and it's raining inside
thoughts skidding
on the wet tarmac
to nowhere.

Words lash backwards
and forwards like storm trees
weak-rooted
falling in the way.

Nothing can get past
I switch the engine off
light a cigarette.
It glows

deep deep down inside
the dark recess of my brain
where sad music plays
of lost love.

It is the only way out
from this driving guilt
and although it will burn
blister my skin

I know that in the morning
when I prick it open
my dark grief will burst out
and daylight rush in.

THE LEFT HAND OF DARKNESS

Night has come
and we have fallen into bed
and my right hand caresses you.
It is an easing of the day
muscles relaxing
heart working in a different way
blood flowing warmly.
But there is a left hand of darkness
and it prods your memory
strokes up lasting worries
pinches a nerve here and there
and soon you are tense
and rigid
can't relax
can't sleep.
Let me hold your hand
push away that sinister left one.
But no
it won't go.
Night can seem everlasting.
But nevertheless we put our hands together
praying for morning
and when it comes
reach out with them
for the warming comfort
of the sun.

SLEEP RUSTLING

so thin skinned
you lie in bed
seeing the darkness
through your eye lids
convinced it's peering in at you
breaking and entering your mind
to burgle all your thoughts
and sell them on
into the public domain

OWL

I saw the best predators of my generation destroyed by pesticides,
naked hysterical poison
dragging themselves through the negro nights at midnight looking
for an angry fly
angle-headed hooters burning for the ancient heavenly connection
to the
starry glow-worm in the machinations of the night
who hungry and terrifying and evil-eyed and on high sat up
looking into the
supernatural darkness of cold wintry clouds
floating across the tops of
hills contemplating nemesis, who bared their claws to heaven on
hell and saw moth-angels staggering over barn roofs illuminated
who passed through the firmament with radiant cool eyes
hallucinating Buckingham-
shire and Blake-like tragedy amongst the spoils of war
who were expelled from the day schools of predatory for the crazy
and regurgitating obscene pellets of
little skeletons and skulls of birds
who glowered in unglazed windows burning their eyesight in
dreams and listening to terror in flashbacks
who got busted on recollections returning through the ether
with a beak of feathers
who ate fireflies in lightning or drank gnat blood in
thunderstorms, death defied or committed purgatory with their
bowelled night after night
with killing, with sacrifice, with sleep-inducing nightmare attacks,
having a ball with blood
incomparable blind attacks of shuddering ferocity, in reality

leaping towards their prey instigating terror
in the motionless time between life and the dawn of cemetery
the neon eye blinking traffic-light moon and tree vibrations
in the winter dusks of England, hoot ranting and satanic
in the shuddering mouth-wracked battered bleakness
in the dream light of swooping oblivion.

AFTER EATING GRASSHOPPERS IN CHELSEA

Dreams packed with protein
a chirping in the ears
with midges swarming beneath the lids of sleep
grasshoppers jumping on your tongue
the crispy chewing of insects crunching in the ears
locusts eating up all taste of disgust
red ants crawling up the left nostril
an earwig in the eye
the leather jacket of a beetle
with bloody cochineal splattered on its sleeve
glow-worms amongst the cobwebs of your brows
cuckoo-spit on eye-lashes
spider filaments hanging from your nose
moths dusting your hair with their debris
snails smearing you with garlic butter
a bluebottle crawling up your thigh
a slug in the navel
breasts swarming with greenfly
a ladybird on your nipple
leeches sucking at your lipstick
caterpillar-blood running down your cheeks
and with thoughts turning to insecticide
you reach for the aerosol that isn't there.

EROGENOUS

after the darkness
the silent waiting
in tunnels

you lay in state
on the hotel bed

letting the shock
of a bomb scare
sweat like nitro-glycerine
from shocked limbs

I recall leading you
out onto the platform
and up along passageways
to ground level

taking you across
taxi-beetled streets
easing you up the stairs
through the bedroom door

where you rapidly took off
all your clothes
like they were soaked in picric acid
ready to explode

I still have my day ticket
ALL ZONES AVAILABLE it says....
a memento of the day
I first saw you naked and afraid

GRACKLE

Nightmares have made an umbrella
from a hundred crows,
pecked fat, wet worms from out a plague of rain.
The beak, the yellow bone,
digs sore into my handle hand
and the word "why?" hops about in my dark, treetop mind.

All is black, and yet no sharps,
though the magpie is blessed with a full keyboard.

No candelabra, brassy, family tree for me,
in which to build a rookery-house of dreams,
or a taking to the raven Tower, to breed
more ravens, lest I begat a Cornish Chough.

It is a black, black rain that falls on down,
that fledgling ancestor of feathers,
but time will be its spokesman,
cover it with a waterproof identity,
launch it from obscurity, extinction,
make it a cover-all, a dry eye,
held under the edge of tearfulness,
a blinking scavenger for life.

To fly above all this would be my dream.
I long all night to be an eagle.

DREAM PLAY FOR INSOMNIACS

Once I dreamt about the normal
and I couldn't stay asleep
leapt up to write it down
and put it in a book
but then the reader
a man called Strindberg
said "No good!
Where are all the severed heads
the men that give birth to horses
and the lobsters endowed with testicles
that inhabit real peoples' dreams?
This is pure fantasy to me."
Yet when I really woke up
and not just in the dream
I remembered the heads
the horses and the testicles
but couldn't recall the man's name.

BLACK MIRROR OF DREAMS

Black mirror of dreams
this is a tour
behind the house-fronts
the shop-windowed daytime
Here is the cracked plaster
the peeling paint of privacy
the yard full of broken promises
the rusting achievements of the past
A near-starving dog
is chained six inches short of food
howls like a thorned foot
realisation shivering
in the shrinking belly
of his most recent opportunity

CANDY STRIPED ENCOUNTERS

We have bodies in the bed
that are well on the way
to getting to know each other
while our pillowed heads
have yet to introduce ourselves.
Our hands are down there too
helping with the puppetry
getting the gloved crocodile
to show its teeth
the skeleton to rattle
while outside the bedroom door
Toby the dog is howling to come in.

STAY WITH ME TILL MORNING

Now that I've found you
the ideal word
the perfect line
do not disappear in my dreams
before I write you down
but stay with me
stay with me till morning.

PASSING THE NIGHT

an imaginary man
with his dog
down by the foggy river
unclear where exactly
but there's a steel bridge
overhead
and the rattling
of invisible rolling stock
another land
or maybe a large ship
with a row of dim lights
lies across the pea-soup waters
and a muffled horn
blows like an animated snore
eyelids sticking together
vision misty
I go to the bathroom
pull the chain silently

MOON IN DUNE

Night, and the lunar seas
lap-in upon another beach
as ancient stars wink down
upon young blonde ones
that lie fish-naked on black sands
dyed secret by the absence of the light.

There they love up a squirm
like net-caught glistening sprats
imprisoned with rampant electric eels
calling out their gulled needs
before, merging crab-like,
and interned, they integrate.

Satisfied, another teenage crush
her rock-pool eyes blind with ecstasy
their lashes stiff tentacles
like paralysed anemones
he lively as a porpoise
showing off his flips.

And later…
the whole beach lit
by the red glow
of post-coital
filter-tips.

NIGHT IS DRAWING IN (ITS LITTLE BLACK BOOK)

Day is night sleeping with the light on;
sometimes you can hear it snoring in the long grass
or find it in windowless rooms,
but mostly it slumbers in a state of invisibility.
By closing your eyes, you can glimpse
into its bedroom,
but you can't put your hand on its shoulder.
Night is not a solid sleeper,
and it doesn't wear a nightshirt or pyjamas,
but sleeps in the Blind Man's buff.
Neither is it a shift worker.
Night works in the dark,
enjoys its breakfast when day is having its supper,
prefers the moon to the sun,
and doesn't have to put up with the crowds like daytime does.
It shares its time with moths, glow-worms, and creepy-crawlies,
badgers, burglars, and owls
and things that rustle in the undergrowth,
but it is not really gregarious,
and it doesn't ever go to Night Clubs
or take a day out somewhere.

SUBMAXIMAL RESPONSES

Sleep is my submarine
takes me down
below the illuminated periscope walls of my retina memories
to where fearsome creatures roam
with their phosphorescent head probes
and albino eyes
to seek answers to the unfathomable.
But when I tug on the line
while images are clear
nobody winds me up
and findings flounder in the ocean space of time
that nitrogen has to flood my blood
with bends and other intricacies
meanderings of truth
that when I reach the shore of day
come mumbo-jumbo out
destroy the truth
its depth charged night rate
and held back until next shift

KEEPER'S LODGE

with the full moon
blowing against the windowpane
green light filtered through yew trees
basking on the wallpaper
sending stripes into hiding
in the shadows
and the starved mirror
inventing images of absent faces
to threaten you
with their tight-lipped demands
you shrink-wrap your fear
in a nylon quilt
of self-preservation.

THE GRIFFITH PLANETARIUM, HOLLYWOOD

(Where James Dean had his tire slashed and fought
The Toughs)

The stars in here
are brighter than those outside
and I am centre of the universe

ST**

He has a flare for burning through the night.
A blue dwarf luminescent, he asterisks the velvet dark****
with his person*****,
his broad grin teeth*** a meeting,
eyes glist***** like diam****.
To all the bright young things,
he is a st**.

BECAUSE THE NIGHT IS MADE FOR LOVERS

Because the night is made for lovers
I meet the others
in the afternoons
when the moon's influence has waned
and lust alone reigns
behind the drawn curtains of suburban rooms
It's an occasion where even *hello*
is just a token
sometimes it's furtive
sometimes it's open
with women free
and women bespoken

PIECE WORK

on the night shift
during tea break
amongst the noise
of love's machinery
you pull the levers
press the buttons
tease their metal
pretend it's a joke
just having a laugh
but desire is there
waiting naked
beneath your
overall

PERDITION

Silver-point on black
the moonstruck hillside
glistens diamond-cut
with long summer grass
its trees stunted
by distance
leaves gleaming intaglio
against the shadowed
darkness
where a woman
in off-shoulder gown
of white
a bouquet of snowdrops
heads down
clasped behind her back
walks alone
on her wedding night

LAMBLAST

The corn is green in the lunar light
its ears cocking their heads
towards you
as you walk midnight
between the rows.
But all is silent
except the beating in your breast
as you approach your farmhouse home
its bleak headstone prominence
as hard as granite
against a slate night-sky
the cold candle light
flickering in a kitchen window
silhouetting the dark shadow
of your lord and master.

SPELLBOUND

Witches it's said
three of 'em
can't sleep
gone from the village
across the field
to the clump of trees
that surround the pond
next to where the young farmhand
used to live
his cottage all in ruins now
standing there
in the flimsiest of nylon
backed by moonlight
their reflections silver
along with the drowning trees
in the black depths that hide
the body of the man
that they took
and drowned
and come now to croak
their evil laughter over
at full moon
each one a sought child of his
tucked up back home
and safe in bed.

HOODLUM LIGHT

At night
out of my window
the sea is menacing.
I see it smoking a cigarette
beneath the pier
its hat pulled down over its brow
wondering if it can break in now
its green eye sussing me.
Something is sticking out
in its pocket
and it's not just pleased to see me.
I imagine it strutting across the street
and beating down my door
surging up the stairs
cold, black and swirling
and demanding that I accompany it
to the nearest hole in the wall
its steel against my back
the salt of fear burning in my throat
a dampness spreading in my trousers.
Out there it is cloning itself
ganging up for the off
while my heart beats a storm warning
calls out for men in yellow oilskins
to come to my rescue
as I plunge my head
beneath the raging sheets
all sticky with dread
and shouting oblivion

and I wonder how long I can hold my breath
a moth-like albatross
circling the dim light
waves of fear
sweeping me near to tears.

ON LUMB BANK, AN EVENING SEMINAR

I see you lingering in first failing of the light,
for dark to fall;
your call not like dove, but snipe.
Claws drawn, teeth bared, you await the night.

You hunt with nocturnal beasts; you have their sight.
The trees are tall,
the midnight pickings ripe.
I see you lingering in first failing of the light.

Fixed in your staring eyes, they give no fight,
the kill is all,
the head, its bloody caul,
feels only the first bite.
I see you lingering in the first failing of the light,
for dark to fall.

MOON LANDING IN MERIONETH-SHIRE

How slate-grey was my valley
the black-eyed houses
caught mouths open
blank faces of the tomb stones
staring
broken-off backdrop of Cader Idris
smouldering on the horizon
all Corris Uchaff seemingly empty
next to a quarry full of darkness
and trees running from the woods
with their arms in uproar
shouting *Go away!*
as the moon swelled in the sky
like the Hindenberg about to explode
and an owl hooted like a referee
indicating stop, offside.
But it came on and on
and would have filled all the heavens
had not a sharp star burst it
with a bang that could be heard
by Mrs. Jones lying in her earplugs
next to the snoring vicar.
And then the sky frowned and spat
and the rain came down loud and oily
on the sleeping windows
the wind lifting tiles
and smashing them like crocks
fallen from a rickety Welsh dresser.
Witches from the hills whistled down the chimneys.
And children pulled the bedclothes over their frightened heads.

WAKE UP CALL

Each night you wake me up
your heart a two-timing cuckold clock
that beats aloud against my naked chest
as you dream about your lover being next
to you and on the hour shriek
and call his name aloud
your whole being sitting up
a moan of ecstasy going through your frame
as I lie there disturbed
one hand on midnight the other
jerking alarmingly around the clock
towards your next undisciplined outburst.

LARK RISING OVER CANDLEWICK

This morning
the sun came up
in the mirrored window
of my youth
and young again and roused
after an illness of age
as there you were
sitting on the bedside of my mind
in the naked light
the shape to come for
like a warm dream
taking its stockings off
and turning its smile to me
the years soaked away
from my loins.

ANOTHER UGLI MORNING

Sugar-iced with the morning frost
the grapefruit moon
its skin orange-peeled with volcanoes and craters
dwarfs the tiny cherry-red sun
as overslept and bleary
it breakfasts to a dawn chorus
from the radio
looming up at my window
like the blind eye of some nightmarish giant
that forgot to die when I stopped dreaming
a huge gallstone rolling about in my mind
as I try to separate the reality of bacon and egg
from the willow patterned plate
of Eastern mythology

NOCTURNE FOR G (MAJOR)

On the telephone this morning
you expressed the fear
that you may be a sleepwalker
having woken up
with grass on your nightdress
and I on my part
refrained from reporting
that last night
I dreamt of taking you
from your bed
and leading you asleep
into the wide open fields
that surround my desires
and laying you down
next to my midnight fantasies.

EACH MORNING LIGHT

Naked you are as complex as calculus
And yet so easily differentiated
Because it is a nakedness
That I have come to know
So that my mind calculates the area beneath the curve
Without but a thought
And tells me in the darkness
That it is you.

Naked you are the coast of my intentions
My passport to abroad withdrawn
My heart confined to house arrest.
Statements that I make
Are vetted by my love for you
Yet prisoner of conscience
I am provided with all the comforts
Wished from life.

Naked you say you love me
It is a statement without clothes.
It smells of your skin.
It throws its arms around my neck.
It is as warm as your body.
I stroll around it all my island day.
And after the lonely tide of sleep
It is the sunshine finger writing in my sand.

DAYTIME WHEN IT PUTS ITS CLOTHES ON

From your patterned coffee mug,
iced with veins that are the same blue
as your skin-silk dressing gown,
you sip your coffee-milk,
fresh from its frothy-laced,
frilly-edged sojourn into the micro-wave,
its *Sweetex* spumed-edge
cauling your tongue with caffeined-casein
as the warmth of its ingestion
migrates to your skin.
I read to you,
a short story by Brautigan,
a meagre page that is a long seductive paging
of the memory
of women when they put their clothes on
in the morning.
And, eyes closed, you are listening
as I gently clothe the naked mind
of early morning
with silk-skinned words
that slide so easily
over the smooth skin of waking,
a waking to the warmth of the sun
on the windows,
the chirping of songbirds
practising their scales,
the taste of milky coffee,
of milky coffee,
that feeling.....
that feeling.....

BLACK BOX

after the gone-out tide of day
the mind walks sideways
in the crab-apple woods
a riddle of twigs sifting the moonlight
onto the badgered undergrowth

and the rippling bed of stones
gurgles with a stream of juicy night thoughts

that illuminate the bat-black cockpit velvet
as the autopilot flies us through our sleep

we are told that the insanity of it
keeps us sane

and despite the fact that flights of fancy
have no parachutes and there is a real danger
of crashing out of this world
into the next

every morning so far
I have awoken to count myself amongst
the survivors

SURVIVING ANOTHER NIGHT

Soaking through the bandages
the suppurating sun
smears its pus across the Earth's horizon
as gangrenous the planet gags
on its own stench
and there is a knowing look of strained horror
on the face of the departing moon
a recollection of its own amputation, long ago.

SOLARGRAPH

Before breakfast
the view squints with anorexia
trees slim to slender verticals
in the sudden brightness of the morning sun
a man's head becomes a matchstick
his body a pair of shoulders on a pin
mountains concave
horizons contract
clouds implode
and sensitive dreams etch
the eyelids of late sleepers
with the bones
of starved lovers
Only the smell of bacon cooking
can fatten light

BREAKFAST AT THE KILDONIAN HOTEL

Ailsa Craig
out there on the Wedgewood sea
working on the eyes geometrically
an equilateral triangle of granite
piercing the misty albumen of sunny sky
from a laid-out Atlantic tablecloth
where the white salt tower
of Pladda island's light sits
as coffee stirs the nostrils
and contentment spreads my toast

RE-ENTRY AFTER INFLUENZAL EXCLUSION

This morning I got up
and scraped a century from my face
outside the sun called relentlessly
like an interrogator's lamp
and my eyes dumbly not answering
I stumbled blindly
down the dishevelled street.

WHEN IT'S ALL OVER WILL YOU BE WITH ME?

When it's all over
will you still walk through the darkness
like an infra-red image
developing on the bromide of my dreams?
Will I see you though I cannot see you
your body displacing space in line with shape
distorting my brain with the anticipation?
Will you lift the lid
like you lifted the sheet
and slide in
seeking warmth from me
and giving it to me
grasping my leg between your thighs
putting your cold nose in my ear?
Will you gasp
when you encounter cold bones
where my flesh used to be?
Will I know you are always next to me
or will death be the end of us?

Indigo Dreams Publishing
132, Hinckley Road
Stoney Stanton
Leicestershire
LE9 4LN
www.indigodreams.co.uk

Papers used by Indigo Dreams are recyclable products made from wood grown in sustainable forests following the guidance of the Forest Stewardship Council.